FAITH
FOUNDATIONS

BUILD YOUR LIFE,
MAKE IT COUNT

DAVID PLATT

ISBN 979-8-9855655-5-3

Published by Radical, Inc.

CONTENTS

INTRODUCTION

In previous books I have written, I have had a relatively narrow audience in mind, specifically the people who live in the country and context where I have served as a pastor. This one is different. Though I believe and hope it will be helpful for those I pastor, I have written this book for people in any country or context in the world. Regardless of where you reside, how young or old you are, and what you're walking through, I've tried to write with you in mind.

I've also kept this book intentionally short so that it might not just be read, but reflected upon. I have tried to include Scripture throughout, and I encourage you to stop and soak in God's Word whenever you see it. In addition, I have included questions at the end of each chapter for contemplation and discussion. I believe you will get the most out of these pages by taking the time to meaningfully answer those questions, ideally in community with others. And if in the end you believe this would be a helpful resource for you to lead others through in order to introduce them to the foundations of following Jesus, then I encourage you to do so.

My sincere hope and prayer is that God will use this book not only to provide you with a clear understanding of the foundations of following Jesus according to his Word, but also to provoke in you an unwavering resolve to experience the life that truly counts in this world.

01
ENJOY AND EXALT

01
ENJOY AND EXALT

My assumption is that you want your life to count for what matters most. I'm assuming you don't want to get to the end of your journey here, look back, and realize, "I missed the point." But if we're not careful and intentional, that's exactly what will happen.

To put my cards on the table from the beginning, I am a Christian—a follower of Jesus. But I want to be clear that I'm not saying that only non-Christians are missing the point of why we're here. I actually believe that in addition to non-Christians, most Christians are missing the point of why we're here. I believe that most people (Christians and non-Christians) are missing the foundational purpose of their lives.

I realize that's a strong statement. I'll be the first to admit that it sounds (and feels!) pretty bold—even offensive—to say to most people, "You're missing the point of life, and if you want your life to count for what matters most, you need to make some major changes."

But that's why I've written this book. I want to show you a concise summary not of what *I* think about the purpose of your life, for that would be a waste of your time. Instead, I want to show you what *God* says about the purpose of your life. To make sure that's the case, test everything I say to see if it aligns with God's Word. And if it does, then I want to challenge you to ask yourself, "Does my life truly align with the purpose for which God has made me?"

For non-Christians, I believe the answer will be, "No." My aim is to show you that you are made for relationship with the God who created you. That relationship is only possible through faith in Jesus, so apart from following him, you will miss the point of your life.

At the same time, for many Christians I believe the honest answer will also be, "No, my life is not aligned with the purpose for which God made me." Or at least, "Not completely." This is because there are some essential foundations of faith in God that, for a long time, we have either unintentionally missed or intentionally ignored, or maybe we've just grown accustomed to a counterfeit version of Christianity that's most acceptable in the culture around us. I have written before about how Christians, specifically in my country, the United States, are tempted to settle for a subtly yet dangerously Americanized version of the gospel that leads to a nice, comfortable Christian spin on the American dream, when in reality we have been created by God for a much bigger dream than this.

In this short book, I want to show you that dream and invite you to live for it. It's a dream that transcends countries and cultures, and once you're captivated by it, you won't want to live for anything less than it. And once that happens, you'll come to the end of your life and conclude by God's grace, "My life here counted for what mattered most."

MADE FOR RELATIONSHIP

The Bible is the supernaturally inspired Word of God, and it reveals who God is and how God has designed us to live. One way to learn what a book is about is by reading its bookends—its beginning and end. So let's look at the bookends of the Bible and see if we can identify God's purpose for our lives in this world according to his Word.

The first chapter of the Bible, Genesis 1, tells the story of creation, including people. The first mention of human beings is in Genesis 1:26–28, where we read,

Then God said, "Let us make man in our image, after our likeness. And let them have dominion over the fish of the sea and over the birds of the heavens and over the livestock and over all the earth and over every creeping thing that creeps on the earth." So God created man in his own image, in the image of God he created him; male and female he created them. And God blessed them. And God said to them, "Be fruitful and multiply and fill the earth and subdue it, and have dominion over the fish of the sea and over the birds of the heavens and over every living thing that moves on the earth."

This account of the creation of man and woman is astounding. Unlike anything else in all the world, you and I—along with every other human being in the history of the world—are made in the image of God. That means you and I have the unique capacity to know and enjoy God in a personal relationship with him. You and I have the extraordinary ability to talk and walk with God himself. Mountains, oceans, stars, planets, plants, and animals cannot do that. Neither can anything we make, including machines or computers, no matter how much artificial intelligence they have. Only human beings made in the image of God can experience personal relationship with God.

From the very beginning of the Bible, God is making clear why he made you and me. To make this specific to your life, **you are made to enjoy God in all of his glory.** The highest purpose of your life is to experience the thrill of a relationship with your Creator characterized by pleasure and love.

Just to make sure we're not reading too much into these initial verses of the Bible, fast-forward to when Jesus, God in the flesh, is asked the question, "Out of all the commandments in the Word, which one is most important?" Jesus answers in Matthew 22:37–38:

You shall love the Lord your God with all your heart and with all your soul and with all your mind. This is the great and first commandment.

Is this not breathtaking? God, the most holy, beautiful, glorious, magnificent, majestic, all-powerful, infinitely-satisfying Being in all the earth, has created you and me to experience life in a love relationship with him. This is why Jesus later prays to God the Father in John 17:3, saying,

And this is eternal life, that they know you, the only true God, and Jesus Christ whom you have sent.

Full life is found in personally knowing the one true God.

THE GREATEST NEWS IN THE WORLD

Now the last part of John 17:3 is extremely important because all of us have run from this relationship with God. It looks different in each of our lives, but we have all sinned against God, turning from his ways to our ways and trusting in ourselves more than him. Our sin has separated us from relationship with God, and if we die in this state of separation, we will spend all of eternity experiencing God's just, holy judgment for our sin away from enjoyment of him.

But the gospel—what the Bible calls the "good news"—is that despite our sin against God, God loves us and has made a way for us to be restored to relationship with him. God has done the unthinkable by coming to us in the person of Jesus. Jesus is God in the flesh, and he came to the world and lived the life none of us could live—a life of no sin. Then, even though he had no sin for which to die, Jesus chose to die on a cross to pay the price for our sin. Jesus died the death we deserve to die. The good news keeps getting better, though, because Jesus didn't stay dead for long. Three days later, Jesus rose from the grave, conquering the enemy we could not conquer: death itself.

As a result of Jesus' death and resurrection, anyone anywhere, no matter who you are or what you have done, can be reconciled to God. If you will turn from your sin and yourself and trust in Jesus as the Savior of your sin and Lord of your life, God will forgive you of all your sin and restore you to relationship with him now and for all of eternity.

Jesus put it this way in John 3:16, likely the most well-known verse in the Bible:

For God so loved the world, that he gave his only Son, that whoever believes in him should not perish but have eternal life.

As part of the world, put your name in that sentence above. God so loves *you* that he gave his only Son for *you*, so that when *you* believe in Jesus, *you* will not experience eternal death, but *you* will experience eternal life in relationship with God.

You and I are made to know, love, experience, and enjoy God in all of his glory, and nothing in this world will ever be able to satisfy you apart from your Creator. Blaise Pascal once described the empty, endless quest for satisfaction in a person's life apart from God this way:

This he tries in vain to fill with everything around him, seeking in things that are not there the help he cannot find in those that are, though none can help, since this infinite abyss can be filled only with an infinite and immutable object; in other words by God himself.

As long as any one of us is separated from God, we will miss the ultimate—and eternal—satisfaction designed for us in God. If you have never truly begun a relationship with God through Jesus, I invite you to pause and pray now for God to forgive you of your sins through faith in Jesus and restore you to relationship with him.

Then once you do, and for all who have, live for this purpose every day: to know, love, experience, and enjoy God in all of his glory. And as you do, realize that as important as this is, if you stop here, you will still miss the purpose of your life.

A WORLDWIDE DREAM

This is where part of the problem lies, and it's why most Christians (i.e., people who have placed their faith in Jesus as Savior and Lord) are still missing out on the purpose of their lives.

If you were to ask the average Christian to summarize the message of Christianity, you would most likely hear something along the lines of, "The message of Christianity is that God loves me." Or similar to the language of John 3:16, someone might say, "The message of Christianity is that God loves me enough to send his Son, Jesus, to die for me."

But let's think about this language and ask, "Is it complete?" Because if the message of Christianity is primarily, "God loves me," then who is the object of Christianity?

God loves *me*.
Me.
Christianity's object is *me*.

Therefore, when I think about *my* faith, I think about *my* life, *my* plans, and *my* dreams. I want to choose what works best for *me*. Even when I think about church, I want to be in a setting that's comfortable for and caters to *me*. Essentially, I create a version of Christianity that revolves around *me*.

But is this biblical Christianity?

Look back at John 3:16. Yes, you and I are included in the world that God loves, but we're clearly not the only ones God loves. God loves everyone in the world this way. God's purpose doesn't just revolve around *me*; it revolves around the *whole world*.

That takes us back to Genesis 1. Do you remember what God said right after he made man and woman in his image? Genesis 1:28 says,

> God blessed them. And God said to them, "Be fruitful and multiply and fill the earth. . . ."

God made us for a love relationship with him, then he said, "Fill the earth with more men and women made in my image who are enjoying me in all of my glory." Apparently, God's purpose for our lives doesn't center around *you* or *me*. Instead, God's purpose for our lives centers around spreading his glory across the earth.

In other words, the message of Christianity is not just, "God loves me." Although that is true, it's incomplete. The message of Christianity is, "God loves me so that I might make him known in all of his glory and love all over the world." To use our language from earlier, according to God's Word, **you are made to enjoy God in all of his glory and exalt God in all of the nations.** Indeed, none of us is made for an American dream, an African dream, a European dream, an Asian dream, or an Australian dream. Instead, you have been made for a worldwide dream—to spread the glory and love of God among all the nations.

THE TRAIN OF HISTORY

This makes sense in light of the second most important commandment Jesus gave us. After Jesus said that "the great and first commandment" is to "love the Lord your God with all your heart and with all your soul and with all your mind," he said,

And a second is like it: You shall love your neighbor as yourself. On these two commandments depend all the Law and the Prophets. (Matthew 22:39–40)

God's love clearly isn't intended to center on us; it's intended to spread to others through us. And not just to the neighbors who are most like us. When Jesus explains this commandment to a lawyer in Luke 10, he makes clear that our neighbors include people from all nations.

That leads us to the last book in the Bible. We said we'd look at the Bible's bookends for clues to what God's Word is about, so let's jump to the end of Scripture. There we see a powerful picture of where all human history is headed. In Revelation 7:9–10, we read,

After this I looked, and behold, a great multitude that no one could number, from every nation, from all tribes and peoples and languages, standing before the throne and before the Lamb, clothed in white robes, with palm branches in their hands, and crying out with a loud voice, "Salvation belongs to our God who sits on the throne, and to the Lamb!"

God has designed all of human history to climax in a countless multitude of men and women enjoying him in all of his glory and exalting him from all the nations, tribes, peoples, and languages of the world.

If this is God's ultimate purpose for all of world history, then clearly this is God's ultimate purpose for our lives in this world. If the train of history is headed toward a multitude of men and women enjoying God in all of his glory and exalting him from all of the nations, and if you want your life to count in this world, then your life should be on this train.

FOR CONTEMPLATION AND DISCUSSION

Take a moment to imagine what a life would look like that is completely consumed with this purpose: enjoying God in all of his glory and exalting God among all the nations. List, and ideally discuss with others, various ways that someone who wants to make their life count for this purpose might use their time, money, and skills. Describe how they might relate to God and other people. Identify the plans and dreams they might have.

Then answer the following question:

Is what you imagined truly what your life looks like today?

02
SUPER
NATURAL
POWER

02
SUPERNATURAL POWER

For far too long, professing Christians have minimized the power of the gospel—the good news of Jesus. Many people who claim to have faith in Jesus basically think, "I've placed my faith in Jesus and I'm for-given of my sin, so now I can just coast things out from here. I'll go to church (at least sometimes), live a good, decent life, and go to heaven when I die. This is the Christian life."

But the gospel is much better news than this. The gospel is the good news that everyone who trusts in Jesus as their Savior and Lord is not only *forgiven of their sin,* but also *filled with God's Spirit.* Every follower of Jesus has the Holy Spirit of God living inside them. And do you know why God puts his Holy Spirit inside of us?

God puts his Holy Spirit in you to give you supernatural power to experience his ultimate purpose for you. In other words, the Holy Spirit of God empowers you to enjoy God in all of his glory and exalt God among all of the nations. You have otherworldly power to make your life count for what matters most in this world and the world to come.

FREE TO LIVE

Here's how this works. Jesus is the perfect example of a life that counts for what matters most, right? He lived perfectly to enjoy God in all of his glory and exalt God among all of the nations. He loved God wholeheartedly and loved his neighbor selflessly, all the way to dying on the cross to bring salvation to people from all nations. As a result, if we want to live for what matters most, then we need the Spirit of Jesus inside of us to make us more like Jesus every day.

This is exactly what the Holy Spirit does in the Christian's life. The Bible says in 2 Corinthians 3:17–18,

Now the Lord is the Spirit, and where the Spirit of the Lord is, there is freedom. And we all, with unveiled face, beholding the glory of the Lord, are being transformed into the same image from one degree of glory to another. For this comes from the Lord who is the Spirit.

There are a lot of details we could talk about in these verses, but don't miss the big picture. For every follower of Jesus, the Spirit of Jesus lives in you for the purpose of transforming you into the image of Jesus. The Holy Spirit sets you free from sin and yourself so that you can enjoy and exalt God more and more like Jesus every single day.

CONCENTRIC CIRCLES

When I think about the transforming work of the Holy Spirit, I find it helpful to think about each of our lives as a set of six concentric circles starting with one at the center. Picture the innermost circle as **your heart.** When you place your faith in Jesus, God puts an entirely new heart inside you. God describes it this way in Ezekiel 36:26–27:

And I will give you a new heart, and a new spirit I will put within you. And I will remove the heart of stone from your flesh and give you a heart of flesh. And I will put my Spirit within you, and cause you to walk in my statutes and be careful to obey my rules.

This is why the Bible talks about becoming a follower of Jesus as being born again (John 3:8) or becoming a new creation (2 Corinthians 5:17). When you place your faith in Jesus, you receive the Spirit of Jesus and you become an entirely new person. Galatians 2:20 puts it this way:

I have been crucified with Christ. It is no longer I who live, but Christ who lives in me.

As a follower of Jesus, you have an entirely new identity because you have an entirely new person—Jesus, through his Spirit—at the core of who you are. And as a result of his residence in your heart, he begins to transform your life from the inside out.

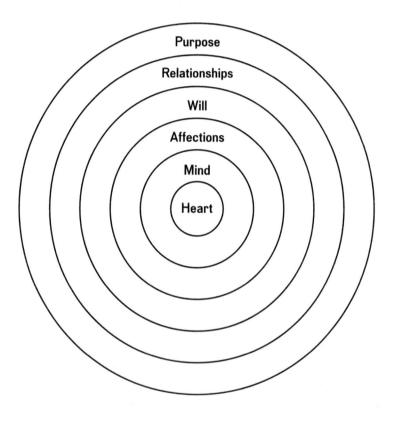

That leads to the next concentric circle: **your mind.** The Spirit of Jesus inside you gradually transforms your mind so that you begin to think more like Jesus. Romans 12:2 says,

Do not be conformed to this world, but be transformed by the renewal of your mind. . . .

As followers of Jesus, we fill our minds with the Word of God, and his Spirit transforms us to think like Jesus.

The next concentric circle is **your affections**, or your desires. The more Jesus transforms your mind about what is good and right, the more you begin to want what Jesus wants and hate what Jesus hates. The Bible says in Psalm 37:4,

Delight yourself in the LORD, and he will give you the desires of your heart.

Sadly, many Christians miss this. They picture Christianity as a list of things to do, and activities like prayer, Bible reading, or gathering for worship with the church feel like boxes to check instead of pleasures to enjoy. And the pleasures they really want are found in all the things they're missing out on in the world.

But this isn't Christianity. Remember that we are created to *enjoy* God in all of his glory. We're not made to pursue God simply because we're supposed to, but sincerely because we want to. We are made to savor the exaltation of God in worship, to crave communion with God in prayer, to hunger for God's Word more than daily food, and to walk in obedience to God because we actually want his ways more than our ways or the ways of this world. All of this happens as the Spirit of Jesus transforms our affections.

As we delight in God's ways, we obey God's will, which leads to the next concentric circle: **your will.** The more we think like Jesus thinks and want what Jesus wants, the more the Holy Spirit helps us to walk as Jesus walked. Jesus makes this connection between his Spirit and our mind, affections, and will in John 14:15–17 when he says,

If you love me, you will keep my commandments. And I will ask the Father, and he will give you another Helper, to be with you forever, even the Spirit of truth, whom the world cannot receive, because it neither sees him nor knows him. You know him, for he dwells with you and will be in you.

Love for Jesus leads us to obedience to Jesus, and it's his Spirit inside of us who aligns our will with his Word.

Think about the relationship between your heart, mind, affections, and will in regard to your struggles with sin. Sin as an act of the will doesn't just appear out of nowhere. It starts with a heart out of tune with God's heart, a mind that believes what isn't true, and affections that are focused on what you want instead of God. Just as Eve ate from the forbidden tree in Genesis 3 because her heart turned from God—she believed the lie that God wasn't good, and she desired that piece of fruit more than she desired God—we sin in similar ways all the time. That means we need God, by his Spirit, to transform us from the inside out (our hearts, our minds, and our affections) if we are going to resist sin (in our actions or in our will).

This leads us to the fifth concentric circle: **your relationships.** The more we live like Jesus lives, the more we will love like Jesus loves. The first word that appears when the Bible describes the fruit of the Holy Spirit in our lives is "love" (Galatians 5:22). This makes sense in light of Jesus' words in John 13:35:

> *By this all people will know that you are my disciples, if you have love for one another.*

This is why followers of Jesus commit their lives to local churches where we love brothers and sisters in Christ like family, and we lay down our lives to serve, help, support, encourage, weep with, rejoice with, care for, and build up one another. As we've been forgiven by God, we forgive others. As we're being served by God, we serve others. This love obviously doesn't stop in our relationships with Christians in our local church or the global church; the Spirit of Jesus inside of us transforms our love for every person in the world.

This leads us not just to the last concentric circle, but to where we began this journey: **your purpose.** Listen to the last words from Jesus to his followers in the book of Matthew (28:19–20):

Go therefore and make disciples of all nations, baptizing them in the name of the Father and of the Son and of the Holy Spirit, teaching them to observe all that I have commanded you. And behold, I am with you always, to the end of the age.

Doesn't that sound like the purpose of our lives? Jesus tells his disciples to exalt God among all the nations by making disciples of all of them, and he tells them that as they do, they will enjoy his presence with them forever and wherever they go. Jesus speaks in a similar way to his followers right before he ascends to heaven in Acts 1:8:

But you will receive power when the Holy Spirit has come upon you, and you will be my witnesses in Jerusalem and in all Judea and Samaria, and to the end of the earth.

Now make the connection between all of these concentric circles. When you place your faith in Jesus, he puts his Spirit inside of you. The Holy Spirit begins transforming you into the image of Jesus from the inside out, changing what you think, what you desire, how you live, and how you love. Ultimately, God's Spirit empowers you to live out God's purpose for you: to enjoy God in all of his glory as you exalt God among all of the nations.

FOR CONTEMPLATION AND DISCUSSION

In light of these concentric circles, take a moment to examine the totality of your life. Ask and answer the following questions:

How do you need the Holy Spirit to transform your **HEART** to be more like Jesus?

How do you need the Holy Spirit to transform your **MIND** to be more like Jesus?

How do you need the Holy Spirit to transform your **AFFECTIONS** to be more like Jesus?

How do you need the Holy Spirit to transform your **WILL** so that you live more like Jesus?

How do you need the Holy Spirit to transform your **RELATIONSHIPS** so that you love more like Jesus?

How do you need the Holy Spirit to transform your **PURPOSE** so that your life is more in line with the purpose of Jesus?

Then pray for the Holy Spirit's help to become more like Jesus in all of these ways.

Refuse to settle for a supposed Christianity that consists of praying a prayer or making a decision at some point in your life and then coasting your way to heaven through casual church attendance and comfortable commitment to Christ on earth. This is not Christianity. Instead, embrace a life of supernatural transformation into the image of Jesus more and more every single day. Experience true Christianity that involves a total revolution of your heart, mind, affections, will, relationships, and purpose, all by the power of God's Holy Spirit living inside you.

03
A NEW IDENTITY

03
A NEW IDENTITY

A disciple-maker. Is that how you would describe yourself?

I think for many Christians, the answer is, "No." For most, this sounds like some other level of Christianity. But according to Jesus, this is foundational to the identity of every follower of Jesus.

Think about Jesus' first words to his disciples in the book of Matthew. Here's how the story goes:

While walking by the Sea of Galilee, he saw two brothers, Simon (who is called Peter) and Andrew his brother, casting a net into the sea, for they were fishermen. And he said to them, "Follow me, and I will make you fishers of men." Immediately they left their nets and followed him. (Matthew 4:18–20)

In the very first sentence Jesus spoke to these disciples, he made clear that every follower of his would be a fisher of men. The imagery was clear to these fishermen: instead of working to bring fish into a net, they would work to bring people into a kingdom.

Then think about Jesus' last words to these same disciples, which we looked at in the last chapter. Before he left them, he told them:

> *All authority in heaven and on earth has been given to me. Go there-*
> *fore and make disciples of all nations, baptizing them in the name of*
> *the Father and of the Son and of the Holy Spirit, teaching them to*
> *observe all that I have commanded you. And behold, I am with you*
> *always, to the end of the age. (Matthew 28:18–20)*

Just as Jesus made clear in the beginning, he was now making clear in the end: to be a disciple of his was to be a disciple-maker of the nations. The conclusion is clear for you and me today: if we are truly following Jesus, we are disciple-makers of the nations.

Doesn't this make sense in light of what we've seen about the purpose of our lives up to this point? We've seen that we are made to enjoy God in all of his glory and exalt God among all of the nations. And we've seen how God puts his Holy Spirit inside of us to empower us to live out this purpose as we become more like Jesus every day. We've also seen that God doesn't just want *us* to enjoy and exalt him by becoming more like Jesus; God wants *more people in more nations* to enjoy and exalt him by becoming more like Jesus.

This means the purpose of our lives is not just to *be* disciples who are enjoying and exalting God, but to *make* disciples who are enjoying and exalting God among all the nations of the world. This is clearly who Jesus has created and called each of us to be: disciple-makers of the nations.

WHO JESUS SAYS YOU ARE

So why do followers of Jesus not see themselves as disciple-makers of the nations? It's almost like we've taken Jesus' command to go and make disciples of all nations and turned it into a suggestion to come and be baptized and sit in one location. This is what many supposed Christians do with their lives. For so many people, Christianity consists of coming to a worship gathering (at least periodically) and maybe even serving in or giving to the church. But we aren't focused on making disciples.

The church is filled with people who've been Christians for 5, 10, 15, 20, 30, 40, or even 50 years who have never led another person to faith in Jesus (especially outside their family) and then shown and taught this new Christian how to follow Jesus in such a way that this new Christian is then leading other people to Jesus. In other words, many Christians are going to stand before Jesus one day, look back at their lives, and realize they didn't do what he left them in this world to do.

Don't let this be your story. You are made for more than this culturally acceptable yet unbiblical brand of Christianity. If you're a disciple of Jesus, the Bible makes clear that you have been saved, called, and empowered by God to be a disciple-maker among the nations. Follower of Jesus, this is who Jesus himself says you are! And what an awesome thought that he says this about you. God has not saved you to sit you on the sidelines of his grand purpose in the world. God has invited you to play a significant part in his plan to reach all the nations of the world with the greatest news in the world.

HOW TO MAKE DISCIPLES

So how? If you were to ask the average Christian sitting in a church service on a Sunday morning to explain how to make disciples of the nations, I think you'd get a variety of jumbled answers and probably a good number of blank stares. Surely this should not be the case when it comes to the one command Jesus gave us before he left the earth.

Based on Jesus' command in Matthew 28, there are four fundamental components of disciple-making. I'll try to summarize them here in a way that will hopefully help you remember them.

SHARE THE WORD

First, we **share the Word**. Just as Jesus said in Matthew 28, we go to people who do not know him and we share the good news of his love for them. Stop and think about the people in your life and sphere of influence who are not followers of Jesus. Making disciples means making the effort to share with them who Jesus is, how much Jesus loves them, and what Jesus has done to make a way for them to have eternal life in relationship with God. This is where disciple-making starts: by going to people and sharing God's Word with them. But it's not where disciple-making stops.

SHOW THE WORD

As disciple-makers of the nations, we also **show the Word**. In Matthew 28, Jesus tells us to baptize people in the name of the Father, the Son, and the Holy Spirit. Think about why it's so important that Jesus would include this here. Baptism symbolizes a person's public, physical identification with Jesus and his church. In baptism, we show the world a picture of the life, death, and resurrection of Jesus. In addition, we baptize people as part of the church, the body of Christ, where we share life in Jesus with one another and show the life of Jesus to one another.

This is fundamental to disciple-making. We don't just lead people to Jesus and then leave them to figure out the Christian life on their own. No, we lead them to identify with Jesus and his church, where they can see his life up close and personal in other Christians. Paul writes in 1 Corinthians 11:1,

Be imitators of me, as I am of Christ.

Disciple-making means showing people the life of Jesus in action in such a way that if they were to imitate your life, they would be imitating Jesus.

TEACH THE WORD

That leads to the next way you make disciples: you **teach the Word.** Jesus tells us to teach others everything he has commanded us, but as soon as we hear Jesus mention "teaching," many of us immediately think, "I'm not a preacher," or "I don't have the gift of teaching, so this is not for me." Yet while the Bible does talk about a gift of teaching and a calling to teach for some people, the Bible also talks about all of God's people passing on his Word to others.

This is the way God (through Moses) puts it when talking to his people in Deuteronomy 6:6–9:

And these words that I command you today shall be on your heart. You shall teach them diligently to your children, and shall talk of them when you sit in your house, and when you walk by the way, and

when you lie down, and when you rise. You shall bind them as a sign on your hand, and they shall be as frontlets between your eyes. You shall write them on the doorposts of your house and on your gates.

These instructions in the Old Testament are the heart behind Jesus' instructions in the New Testament. Jesus is telling us as disciple-makers to constantly pass God's Word on to others in such a way that we help others know it and obey it.

SERVE THE WORLD

Finally, Jesus is telling us to do all of the above (share the Word, show the Word, and teach the Word) in all nations. This means that in disciple-making, we **serve the world**. We'll talk more about this part of disciple-making in the next chapter, but for now, I simply want to stop and ask: how are you making disciples?

FOR CONTEMPLATION AND DISCUSSION

Think about your sphere of influence, including your family, friends, classmates, co-workers, neighbors, and the people around you in your city, in addition to the people who attend your church. Ask and answer the following questions and, if you're willing, discuss them with others:

Who are you intentionally sharing God's Word with?

Who are you intentionally showing God's Word to?

How are you intentionally passing God's Word on to others and helping them obey it?

Then answer and discuss these questions:

How can you more intentionally share God's Word with others?

How can you more intentionally show God's Word to others?

How can you more intentionally pass God's Word on to others and help them obey it?

Don't miss this essential foundation to faith in Jesus. If you
are a follower of Jesus, you are a disciple-maker for Jesus.
God has not created you just for you to enjoy him. If that
were the only reason God made you, then he would immediately bring you to heaven after your salvation so that you
could enjoy him in perfect, full, and final freedom from this
fallen world. But he's not done that yet.

Instead, he's giving you breath right now to enjoy him and
exalt him by growing as a disciple of Jesus and by going
and making disciples of the nations. And as a reminder, he
has put his Spirit inside you to help you do this. You have
supernatural power living in you to love people enough to
lead them to Jesus, even when it's hard, costly, or takes you
out of your comfort zone.

Christian, you are a disciple-maker of the nations. By the
power of his Spirit in us, let's be who Jesus has created us
to be and do what Jesus is commanding us to do.

04
ALL THE NATIONS

04
ALL THE NATIONS

Let's summarize what we've seen in three chapters so far:

1. You are made to enjoy God in all of his glory and exalt God in all of the nations.

2. God's Holy Spirit lives inside every follower of Jesus, transforming you every day from the inside out to become more like Jesus and experience his purpose for your life.

3. Every follower of Jesus is a disciple-maker of the nations, which means you live out God's purpose for your life by sharing, showing, and teaching God's Word as you serve the world.

So what does it mean to *serve the world*? What does it look like to be a disciple-maker *of the nations*? Are each of us as followers of Jesus really supposed to focus on *all nations*? Is the purpose of my life actually a *global* purpose?

ALL THE ETHNIC GROUPS IN ALL THE EARTH
Remember what God said when he created us in Genesis 1. In verse 28, we read the very first words God ever spoke to people:

*And God blessed them. And God said to them, "Be fruitful and mul-
tiply and fill the earth. . . ."*

Now compare these words from God in Genesis 1 to the words
from Jesus we looked at in Matthew 28:19:

Go therefore and make disciples of all nations. . . .

Do you see the similarity? Just as God wanted his image-bearers to
spread his glory across the earth in Genesis 1, Jesus called his disciples
to spread his gospel across all the nations in Matthew 28. It sure seems
like God's purpose for our lives—and especially as followers of Jesus
—is global in nature.

Interestingly, the word Jesus uses for "nations" in Matthew 28:19
is *ethne*, from which we get the term "ethnic groups." Jesus isn't just
referring to "nations" in the sense of countries or geopolitical entities
that exist today. Instead, Jesus is referring to ethnic groups, or groups
of people who share common language or cultural characteristics. It's
similar to the picture we see in Revelation 7:9–10 of a multitude from
every nation, tribe, language, and people.

This is important because while there are approximately 200 countries that we might call "nations" today, there are far more ethnic,
tribal, language, or people groups that exist in the world. Some people
estimate that there are over 11,000 distinct ethnic groups, and others

estimate that there are over 16,000 of them. Regardless of how many of them exist, Jesus has made clear his command for us to make disciples in *all* of them.

KEEP PRESSING ON

This is why we see followers of Jesus doing what they're doing in the book of Acts. As we've already read, right before Jesus ascends into heaven, he tells his disciples in Acts 1:8,

But you will receive power when the Holy Spirit has come upon you, and you will be my witnesses in Jerusalem and in all Judea and Samaria, and to the end of the earth.

Notice the geography in Jesus' words. Jesus says, "Once my Holy Spirit comes upon you, you'll start spreading the gospel and making disciples in Jerusalem." And that's exactly what they did. When the Holy Spirit came upon them, they started witnessing to Jesus, and thousands of people put their faith in Jesus and were baptized. In other words, these followers of Jesus made disciples in Jerusalem, just like Jesus had told them to do.

Then Acts 8:1 tells us what happened after Stephen was stoned for proclaiming the gospel in Jerusalem:

And there arose on that day a great persecution against the church in Jerusalem, and they were all scattered throughout the regions of Judea and Samaria, except the apostles.

Three verses later, Acts 8:4 tells us,

Now those who were scattered went about preaching the word.

The followers of Jesus in the book of Acts are now making disciples (sharing the Word, showing the Word, and teaching the Word) not just in Jerusalem, but in Judea and Samaria.

Then we fast-forward a few more chapters to Acts 11:19–21, and we read this:

Now those who were scattered because of the persecution that arose over Stephen traveled as far as Phoenicia and Cyprus and Antioch, speaking the word to no one except Jews. But there were some of them, men of Cyprus and Cyrene, who on coming to Antioch spoke to the Hellenists also, preaching the Lord Jesus. And the hand of the Lord was with them, and a great number who believed turned to the Lord.

These followers of Jesus were obeying Jesus' command in Matthew 28:19 and fulfilling Jesus' promise in Acts 1:8. They were witnessing about Jesus from Jerusalem to Judea and Samaria to the ends of the earth, not just among Jewish people, but among Greeks also. Disciples were being made among more ethnic groups in more places.

They didn't stop there. These followers of Jesus kept pressing on to new places and people groups where disciples hadn't been made. In Acts 13:1–3, we read,

Now there were in the church at Antioch prophets and teachers, Barnabas, Simeon who was called Niger, Lucius of Cyrene, Manaen a lifelong friend of Herod the tetrarch, and Saul. While they were worshiping the Lord and fasting, the Holy Spirit said, "Set apart for me Barnabas and Saul for the work to which I have called them." Then after fasting and praying they laid their hands on them and sent them off.

As Acts 13 continues, Barnabas and Saul (or Paul) travel from one new city to the next, from Antioch to Cyprus to Pisidian Antioch to Iconium to Lystra to Derbe, and in all of these places, they make disciples and gather them into churches. Then they return to Antioch and report to the church how the gospel is spreading.

Then in Acts 16, the church at Antioch sends Paul out again, this time with Silas and eventually Timothy, and they go and make disciples in more places where the gospel hadn't gone, in cities like Philippi, Thessalonica, Athens, and Corinth. Eventually, disciples of Jesus are made in this entire region, and Paul writes a letter to the church in Rome saying, "Disciples have been made everywhere here, so now we need to press on to new places like Spain where people haven't heard the gospel" (see Romans 15:18–24).

Why are followers of Jesus in Acts working to make disciples in more and more places where the gospel had not gone? Because this is precisely what Jesus had told them to do. When Jesus told them to make disciples of all nations, he wasn't just generally commanding them to make as many disciples as possible wherever they lived. He was specifically commanding them to make disciples among all the ethnic groups in every corner of the earth until every nation, tribe, language, and people was reached with the gospel.

FOR CONTEMPLATION AND DISCUSSION

In the next chapter, we're going to consider the state of disciple-making in the world today. But for now I want to stop and let this soak in, because this is a foundational truth in the Bible that most Christians are completely missing today. Jesus has not just commanded us generally to make a lot of disciples in the world. Jesus has commanded us very specifically to make disciples among every single ethnic group in the world. This means we don't have the option of just making disciples among people who look like us or among people who are close to us. We have been commanded by Jesus to make disciples among every type of person in the world, including people very far from us.

In light of this specific command to make disciples of *all* the ethnic groups of the world, pause and consider and maybe discuss with others the following questions:

In what specific ways does your life currently reflect a focus on making disciples of **ALL NATIONS?**

In what specific ways might God be calling you to put
more focus on making disciples of **ALL NATIONS?**

How does a focus on making disciples of **ALL NATIONS**
affect the way you approach singleness, marriage, and/or
parenting?

How does a focus on making disciples of **ALL NATIONS**
affect the way you approach school, work, and/or
retirement?

How does a focus on making disciples of **ALL NATIONS** affect the plans and dreams you have for your life?

As we answer these questions, the complete picture of the Christian life—the life that counts for what matters most—is beginning to come into view.

05

THE STATE OF THE WORLD

05
THE STATE OF THE WORLD

So how are we doing?

If you and I are made to enjoy God in all of his glory and exalt God among all of the nations, which includes at least 11,000 distinct people groups in the world, how well are we doing in making disciples among them? That seems like an important question for every Christian to ask. If this is the purpose of our lives and the reason Jesus has left us on this earth, then we should know whether or not it's actually happening.

The answer to that question is that as best as we can tell, there are still about 7,000 ethnic groups comprising approximately 3 billion people who haven't been reached with the good news of God's love in Jesus. This seems pretty significant for people who are made to exalt God's glory by making disciples among all 7,000 of those ethnic groups. Doesn't it?

GREEN ZONES AND RED ZONES

Scan the QR code to see a
full color version of this map

GREEN ZONES AND RED ZONES

Let me show you a map with colors on two ends of a spectrum. The lighter areas on this map generally show places in the world that have been reached with the gospel. These are called "green zones." Obviously green doesn't mean that everyone in these areas is a follower of Jesus, but it does mean that disciples have been made and churches have been planted in these green zones, and most people who live there will encounter a Christian at some point in their lives who can share the gospel with them.

The darker areas on this map show places in the world that have not been reached by the gospel. These are called "red zones." There are very few, if any, Christians or churches in these red zones, which means that most people in red zones will likely never at any point in their lives encounter a Christian who can share the gospel with them. Practically, if you live in a red zone, the high probability is that you will be born, live, and die without ever even hearing the good news that God so loved the world that he gave his Son so that whoever believes in him will never perish but have everlasting life.

OVER 3 BILLION

Over 3 billion people live in the red zones of the world. That's a staggering number. What happens to all of those people when they die if they have never heard the gospel? This is an extremely, eternally significant question for those 3 billion people, and for all of us who are created by God to exalt God among them.

The Bible answers this question in Romans 10:13–17. In a letter that Paul writes specifically to mobilize Christians to spread the gospel to people who have never heard it, he says,

For "everyone who calls on the name of the Lord will be saved." How then will they call on him in whom they have not believed? And how are they to believe in him of whom they have never heard? And how are they to hear without someone preaching? And how are they to preach unless they are sent? As it is written, "How beautiful are the feet of those who preach the good news!" But they have not all obeyed the gospel. For Isaiah says, "Lord, who has believed what he has heard from us?" So faith comes from hearing, and hearing through the word of Christ.

In that last verse, God makes clear that people cannot put their faith in Jesus if they never hear the truth about Jesus. Going back to the first verse in this passage, everyone who calls on Jesus as Lord will be saved. But people can't call on Jesus' name if they never hear the good news about him. And they won't hear the good news about Jesus unless someone tells them.

Are we hearing this? People cannot be saved from their sin if they never hear about Jesus, which means that for over 3 billion people in the world, if they die without ever hearing the gospel, then they cannot be saved from their sin. In other words, over 3 billion people in the world at this moment are on a road that leads away from God to an eternal hell, and they cannot experience eternal life in relationship with God in heaven unless somebody reaches them with the gospel.

PRAYING AND GIVING

I pray that this will be an eye-opening moment for you as we approach the halfway point of this journey. You are made by God to enjoy him in all of his glory and exalt him among all of the nations. You are saved by the gospel and called by God to be a disciple-maker of the nations. And you live in a world where over 3 billion people among the nations still haven't been reached with the good news of God's love.

Surely this needs to change. And what we're seeing in God's Word is that every one of us has a part to play in bringing about that change. God has not saved you to sideline you but rather to use you to play a unique and significant part in reaching the nations with the gospel.

God is calling you to pray for the spread of the gospel to all the people groups of the world. Each of us can be a part of what God is doing among red zones anytime and anywhere, including before we even get out of bed in the morning. Just as Jesus taught us to pray for the hallowing of God's name in all the earth (Matthew 6:9), let's pray specifically and intentionally for people to be reached and God to be exalted in the red zones.

Let's give our resources, gifts, time, and money toward this goal. God has given his people wealth unprecedented in the history of the world for the spread of the gospel throughout the world. Yet if you look at our lives, even as Christians, we spend most of our money on ourselves (or keep most of our money for ourselves). On average, we give a small amount of that money to churches or ministries, and we spend most of that money on making church comfortable for ourselves. Then we give a very small percentage of money from churches and ministries to spreading the gospel around the world.

But did you know that out of even that small amount of money that we give to spreading the gospel around the world, about 99% of that money goes to green zones? About 99% of what churches and ministries give goes to places in North and South America, sub-Saharan Africa, Europe, or some parts of Asia that have already been reached with the gospel. It's certainly not wrong to give to gospel work in those places, but we need to open our eyes to this great imbalance: we are giving relative pennies to exalting God among over 3 billion people who have never even heard the good news of his love for them. This is not what it looks like to make our lives count for the purpose for which we're made.

GOING

God is calling us to pray, give, and go and make disciples of all nations. This starts right outside our front doors. In addition to making disciples among people who look or sound like us, just think about how God has brought people from red zones to the neighborhoods and cities where some of us live in green zones. We have abundant opportunities to make disciples of all the nations right where we live.

Then at some point, if the gospel is going to spread to all the red zones in the world, multitudes of people with the gospel are going to need to scatter throughout those red zones. Just like we read about in Acts 8:4 when all the Christians from Jerusalem scattered into Judea and Samaria, over 3 billion people in red zones need not just a few hundred or a few thousand Christians from green zones to go to them, but hundreds of thousands, if not millions, of Christians going to red zones with the gospel. Some will go for a week or two, others will go for a month or year, and some will go for a lifetime to red zones. But every one of us is created and called, whether we're living in green zones or red zones, to be a disciple-maker of the nations.

A UNIQUE MOMENT IN HISTORY

Please pay attention closely to the following two sentences (with a bit of explanation for each of them). First, **there are more people in the world today who have not been reached with the gospel than ever before in history**. The world population is increasing, including among the red zones, which means that during this time that you and I are alive, there are more people than ever before in history who are living, dying, and entering an eternal hell without ever even hearing the good news of God's love for them. This is happening on our watch.

At the same time, second, **we have more opportunities today to reach people in the world with the gospel than ever before in history**. Through travel, we can be almost anywhere in the world in a mere day or two. Through technology, we can communicate with people around the world in real-time in multiple languages through a device we carry in our pockets. The world has become increasingly urban, leading people from ethnic groups to gather in city centers. The migration of people groups in the world to different places is unparalleled in world history. And the globalization of the marketplace makes it possible for the gospel to spread to every corner of the earth on the wings of work.

What a time to be alive! What a time and place for people with a purpose to enjoy and exalt God among all of the nations to be on the earth.

WHAT ABOUT NEEDS IN MY LIFE AND COMMUNITY?

Now you might think, "I see this need in the world, but I have so much going on in my life." And you might even think, "I'm walking through some really hard things in my life or family or work." Or, "I'm surrounded by other people who are walking through hard things. Don't you know there are people in need in the green zones?" With questions like these on our minds, it can be understandably hard to lift your eyes to people far from you who don't have the gospel.

But that's kind of the point. By God's grace, you have the gospel. Amidst all that you are walking through in your life, family, or work, by God's grace, you have the hope, peace, joy, comfort, and knowledge of God's love for you in the gospel of Jesus. You know that trials and suffering will not be the end of your story in this world because you have eternal life in Jesus that transcends this world. And even the people around you who don't believe the gospel have someone who can share it with them.

We're talking about over 3 billion people in the world who are walking through similar trials and suffering (and in many parts of the world, more severe trials and suffering), but they have never even heard of the hope, peace, joy, comfort, and love that are found in God through Jesus. And if nothing changes, eternal suffering will be the end of their story.

So absolutely, press into the gospel of Jesus in your life amidst everything you're facing. And share the gospel of Jesus with the people right around you amidst everything they're facing. And as you do, open your eyes to the historic opportunities you and I have to spread this gospel literally to the ends of the earth in the time and place in which God has put us.

FOR CONTEMPLATION AND DISCUSSION

Over 3 billion people are unreached by the gospel today, and we have created a Christian and church culture in green zones around the world that is practically content to ignore them. The answer to this mammoth problem of unreached people is not just for a few more Christians to become missionaries and take the gospel to them. Instead, the answer is for every single Christian to rise up as a disciple-maker of the nations, living and dying wherever we live (in green zones or red zones) to enjoy God in all of his glory and exalt him among all of the nations.

Consider the part God is calling you to play in this global purpose. Ask, answer, and discuss with others the following questions:

How can you pray daily and specifically for the exaltation of God among all the nations?

How can you spend your resources (including your time, money, and skills) intentionally, generously, and sacrificially for the exaltation of God among all the nations?

How can you go and make disciples of all the nations where you currently live?

What avenues are available to you to go and make disciples in a red zone for a short time and/or for a long time?

If God leads you to live in a green zone, how can you live and work there for the spread of the gospel in red zones?

The reason I encourage you to discuss these questions with others goes back to the essence of disciple-making. The Christian life is not just about you following Jesus; it's about helping others follow Jesus. Making disciples of all nations involves mobilizing others to do the same, so look for opportunities to help other followers of Jesus ask and answer these questions so they can also experience God's purpose for their lives.

06

THE STORY OF GOD'S PEOPLE

06
THE STORY OF GOD'S PEOPLE

For the first 15 years of my Christian life, I filed what we're seeing in this book under the category of "missions" in the Christian life. "Exalting God in other nations"—that's what "missionaries" did. And I was thankful for them. But I wasn't one of them. So it didn't really apply to me.

All of that changed in two particular moments that altered the trajectory of my life when I realized this has been the story of God's people ever since the start of God's people.

NOT FOR YOUR SAKE
The first moment was when I sat with my Bible in a small group of people, and a man showed me a picture I had not seen in all my years of reading God's Word. He showed me how all the books of the Bible connect together to tell one overarching story. And he showed me how my life is a part of that story.

After God made man and woman in his image in Genesis 1, and sin entered the world and God promised to send a Savior in Genesis 3, God called Abraham to be the father of his people in the world. In Genesis 12:1–3, we read,

Now the Lord said to Abram, "Go from your country and your kindred and your father's house to the land that I will show you. And I will make of you a great nation, and I will bless you and make your name great, so that you will be a blessing. I will bless those who bless you, and him who dishonors you I will curse, and in you all the families of the earth shall be blessed."

God called Abraham to enjoy his blessing and to spread his blessing to all the peoples (all the families) of the earth. Not coincidentally, God spoke the same way to Abraham's son, Isaac, in Genesis 26:4:

I will multiply your offspring as the stars of heaven and will give to your offspring all these lands. And in your offspring all the nations of the earth shall be blessed.

Then God spoke the same way to Isaac's son, Jacob, in Genesis 28:14:

Your offspring shall be like the dust of the earth, and you shall spread abroad to the west and to the east and to the north and to the south, and in you and your offspring shall all the families of the earth be blessed.

From the very beginning of his people in the world, God was establishing a pattern of blessing *his* people for the spread of his blessing to *all* peoples.

This pattern continued as God delivered Jacob's descendants from slavery in Egypt. In a stunning display of God's blessing, God split the Red Sea in half and brought his people through on dry land. Why did God bless them like this? Psalm 106:8 tells us:

Yet he saved them for his name's sake, that he might make known his mighty power.

God saved his people in order to make the glory of his name known among all the peoples.

This pattern continues through story after story in the Bible. Think about Shadrach, Meshach, and Abednego in Daniel 3. In another mind-blowing picture of God's blessing, God delivered them from a furnace filled with fire. Why? So that a pagan king named Nebuchadnezzar would declare in Daniel 3:28–29,

Blessed be the God of Shadrach, Meshach, and Abednego, who has sent his angel and delivered his servants, who trusted in him, and set aside the king's command, and yielded up their bodies rather than serve and worship any god except their own God. Therefore I make a decree: Any people, nation, or language that speaks anything against the God of Shadrach, Meshach, and Abednego shall be torn limb from limb, and their houses laid in ruins, for there is no other god who is able to rescue in this way.

The same thing happens three chapters later when Daniel is delivered spectacularly from a den of lions. The Bible records this response from another pagan king named Darius in Daniel 6:25–27:

Then King Darius wrote to all the peoples, nations, and languages that dwell in all the earth: "Peace be multiplied to you. I make a decree, that in all my royal dominion people are to tremble and fear before the God of Daniel, for he is the living God, enduring forever; his kingdom shall never be destroyed, and his dominion shall be to the end. He delivers and rescues; he works signs and wonders in heaven and on earth, he who has saved Daniel from the power of the lions."

God was blessing his people for the spread of his glory among "all the peoples, nations, and languages that dwell in all the earth."

This biblical pattern continues in the building of the temple in the Old Testament. At its dedication, Solomon prayed,

Likewise, when a foreigner, who is not of your people Israel, comes from a far country for your name's sake (for they shall hear of your great name and your mighty hand, and of your outstretched arm), when he comes and prays toward this house, hear in heaven your dwelling place and do according to all for which the foreigner calls to you, in order that all the peoples of the earth may know your name and fear you, as do your people Israel, and that they may know that this house that I have built is called by your name. (1 Kings 8:41–43)

The temple at the center of God's people in the Promised Land was designed to be a grand display of God's glory to all peoples from every land. Similarly, the Psalms portray this theme over and over again, summarized in this prayer in Psalm 67:1–2 that I have prayed over my kids every night I have tucked them into bed:

May God be gracious to us and bless us and make his face to shine upon us, that your way may be known on earth, your saving power among all nations.

There it is: enjoy God in all of his glory (as his face shines upon you!) and exalt God among all of the nations.

This pattern persists throughout all the prophets in the Bible. Ezekiel summarizes it best when he recounts why God blesses his people, saying in Ezekiel 36:22–23,

Therefore say to the house of Israel, Thus says the Lord God: It is not for your sake, O house of Israel, that I am about to act, but for the sake of my holy name, which you have profaned among the nations to which you came. And I will vindicate the holiness of my great name, which has been profaned among the nations, and which you have profaned among them. And the nations will know that I am the Lord, declares the Lord God, when through you I vindicate my holiness before their eyes.

God makes clear in these words that he was blessing his people not ultimately for their sake, but for the sake of his holy name among all the nations. Consider also how God called Jonah the prophet to go to a foreign, enemy nation and proclaim his salvation to them. The heart of God was clearly to bless his people for the spread of his blessing to all peoples, even the unlikeliest of nations.

It's no surprise, then, to turn the pages of the Bible over to the New Testament and see Jesus, once he has made the way of salvation possible through his life, death, and resurrection, saying what we've already seen him say in Matthew 28:19:

Go therefore and make disciples of all nations. . . .

Look closely at Luke's account of that same conversation in Luke 24:46–47, where Jesus tells his disciples,

Thus it is written, that the Christ should suffer and on the third day rise from the dead, and that repentance for the forgiveness of sins should be proclaimed in his name to all nations, beginning from Jerusalem.

According to Jesus in these verses, the invitation to salvation for all the nations is a fundamental part of the gospel message itself. The gospel is not just good news for some types of people; it is good news for every type of person in every nation.

We won't re-trace all that we've already looked at in the New Testament that follows, but as we've seen, the story of the church is the story of proclaiming the gospel, making disciples, and glorifying God among more and more people in more and more places. And it all culminates in Revelation 7:9–10 with a multitude from every nation, tribe, language, and people enjoying and exalting God.

So there I sat in that small group of people, and my jaw was on the ground. For the first time in my Christian life, I realized that this was the foundational story of God's people. God blesses his people through dazzling displays of his love and miraculous demonstrations of his power ultimately not for their sake, but for the spread of his glory among all the peoples of the world. And that's when it hit me. I am counted among God's people. Which means I am blessed by him for this same purpose.

THE PASSION OF ALL GOD'S PEOPLE

This realization went to another level in the days ahead as I learned more about the number of unreached people in the world. At that point, it felt like a no-brainer to me. If this is the big picture story of God's people in the Bible, if the purpose of my life as his child is to enjoy him and exalt him among all the people groups of the world, and if there are people groups in the world who have not been reached with the gospel, then I need to become a missionary in another nation.

That's what my wife, Heather, and I started prayerfully considering for our future. Until one day when I had breakfast with the president of an international missions organization. His name is Jerry Rankin, and the night before I went to breakfast with him, I told Heather, "I'm planning to tell him we want to move to another nation for the spread of the gospel. Is that okay with you?" She said that was great with her, we prayed together the next morning, and off I went.

As soon as we sat down for breakfast, I started pouring out my heart about what I had realized was the big picture story of God's people in his Word and how I wanted to live for God's glory among all the nations. I concluded, "My wife and I are ready to move to another nation."

He looked back at me and for about sixty seconds encouraged me in what I had just shared with him. Then he spent the rest of breakfast talking with me about the need for leaders in the church where the gospel has gone (i.e., in green zones) to mobilize the church to spread the gospel where it hasn't gone (i.e., to red zones).

I was so confused.

I went home to Heather and she excitedly asked me how the conversation went. I told her, "I think the president of this missions organization talked me out of becoming a missionary." Heather's face dropped, almost like I had failed the interview and ruined our dreams for the future.

But looking back, I am so thankful for that breakfast conversation because Jerry Rankin put a category in my mind that didn't exist before that day. Apparently, there is a type of person who is passionate about spreading God's glory among all the nations but who doesn't become a missionary. And the more I thought about it, the more I realized, "Well, of course there's a category for people like that. It's called a *Christian*."

Are missionaries really the only people who are living to see God exalted among all the nations? Where is that in the Bible? From cover to cover in Scripture, from Genesis to Revelation, all of God's people are created to enjoy God's blessing and spread God's blessing among all peoples. This is for all of us.

As we've seen, every Christian has the Holy Spirit, the very Spirit of Jesus, living inside of them. Is the Spirit of Jesus passionate about seeing all nations reached with the gospel? Absolutely, he is. Do you have the Spirit of Jesus in you? If so, then you are passionate about seeing all nations reached with the gospel. This is a fundamental passion for every follower of Jesus.

May God help us—we have taken his ultimate purpose for all of his people revealed throughout his Word and turned it into an optional program for a select few people in the church. According to God's Word, the spread of his glory among all nations is not an optional "missions" program for a few Christians. It's the main purpose for which he has made us.

FOR CONTEMPLATION AND DISCUSSION

God is creating, calling, and blessing his people with salvation for the spread of his glory among all peoples. This is the story of God's Word, and as part of the people of God today, our lives are now caught up in this story.

Up until now, the questions we have asked at the end of each chapter have focused mainly on our individual lives. But in light of what we have seen in the story of God's people throughout his Word, I want to encourage you to ask the following questions and discuss them with others:

What would it look like for a group of people to devote their lives with zeal to enjoying God in all of his glory and exalting God among all the nations together?

What would they do when they gather together?

What would they do when they scatter apart?

How would they work together to make disciples of all nations in ways they could not do alone?

As you answer these questions, I challenge you to consider: Could it be that foundationally this is what the church is supposed to look like in the world according to God's Word?

07

WALKING WITH GOD THROUGH PRAYER AND FASTING

07
WALKING WITH GOD THROUGH PRAYER AND FASTING

One of my favorite verses in the Bible is Genesis 5:24. It tells the short story of a man named Enoch, and the description of his life is shockingly simple. Genesis 5:24 says,

Enoch walked with God, and he was not, for God took him.

Enoch's entire life was summarized in four words: he walked with God.

In a sense, these words are the essence of all we're seeing in this book. We enjoy God in all of his glory as we walk with him. And we exalt him among all nations as he leads us. Experiencing God's purpose for our lives is the overflow of simply walking with God each day.

Over the next two chapters, I want to share with you three foundational disciplines for walking with God. I call these disciplines *foundational* because they open the door to every facet of what it means to enjoy and exalt God. To help you remember them, I'll give you an acrostic for each of them.

PRAY

The first foundational discipline is prayer. Listen to Jesus' words to his followers in Matthew 6:5–15:

> And when you pray, you must not be like the hypocrites. For they love to stand and pray in the synagogues and at the street corners, that they may be seen by others. Truly, I say to you, they have received their reward. But when you pray, go into your room and shut the door and pray to your Father who is in secret. And your Father who sees in secret will reward you.

> And when you pray, do not heap up empty phrases as the Gentiles do, for they think that they will be heard for their many words. Do not be like them, for your Father knows what you need before you ask him. Pray then like this:

> "Our Father in heaven, hallowed be your name. Your kingdom come, your will be done, on earth as it is in heaven. Give us this day our daily bread, and forgive us our debts, as we also have forgiven our debtors. And lead us not into temptation, but deliver us from evil."

> For if you forgive others their trespasses, your heavenly Father will also forgive you, but if you do not forgive others their trespasses, neither will your Father forgive your trespasses.

This is nothing short of awesome. The God who spoke and caused the entire universe to come into being has invited you to get alone in a room with him anytime so that you can experience supernatural reward from him. Then God invites you to leave that room and go into all that life brings in continual conversation with him.

So what is prayer? What do we do when we're alone with God or as we're walking with God throughout the day? Here is an acrostic that answers that question and summarizes how Jesus teaches us to pray in Matthew 6: **PRAY**.

Start with **PRAISE**. Praise God for who he is and thank God for what he has done. Jesus teaches us to pray, "Our Father in heaven." Just think about that. For all who trust in Jesus, the holy, sovereign, all-powerful, all-knowing God over all creation is your Father. You're his child. So spend time praising God for who he is in all of his attributes and thanking God for all he has done and is doing in your life and in the world around you. Spend time at some point in your day alone with God, maybe on your knees, sometimes on your face, sometimes in silence, and other times in singing, pondering who God is and praising him accordingly.

Then let praise lead you to **REPENT**. The more we see who God is in his holiness, the more we see our lack of holiness and our need for his grace. Therefore, spend time in confession of sin. Jesus teaches us to pray, "Forgive us our debts." Examine your life daily. Consider all of those concentric circles in your life: your heart, mind, affections, will, relationships, and purpose. What in any of these areas of your life is not holy and pleasing to God? Confess your sin humbly and honestly before him, knowing that he loves you deeply, forgives you freely, and cleanses you completely.

This dependence on God's grace leads us to **ASK** for God's help in our lives and for others' lives. Jesus teaches us to ask God, "Give us this day our daily bread." In prayer, we look to God for his help and provision on a daily basis. Spend concentrated and continual time throughout your day, saying, "God, I need this. This person needs that." At some point in your day, pray, "God, these people groups in the world need the gospel. Please cause your name to be hallowed there." We have so many things to ask God for in our lives, in others' lives, and in the world, and God our Father has invited us to participate with him in all he is doing in the world by asking and by trusting him with whatever we ask.

Such trust leads us to **YIELD** our lives to God in prayer. Jesus teaches us to say, "Your will be done," and to ask God to lead us into the life he has designed for us. So pray for God to guide your steps and help you to walk closely with him, enjoy him to the full, and exalt him wherever he leads you.

You've been invited by God himself to walk with him in prayer. Make sure you take full advantage of this invitation through concentrated and continual time in prayer in all these ways each day.

FAST

Then notice what Jesus tells his followers right after he teaches them to pray. He says in Matthew 6:16–18,

> And when you fast, do not look gloomy like the hypocrites, for they disfigure their faces that their fasting may be seen by others. Truly, I say to you, they have received their reward. But when you fast, anoint your head and wash your face, that your fasting may not be seen by others but by your Father who is in secret. And your Father who sees in secret will reward you.

Jesus' words are not, "If you fast," but, "When you fast," just like he described prayer. According to Jesus, fasting is just as foundational to walking with God as prayer is.

So how do we fast? Here's another acrostic: **FAST.**

Fasting starts with **FOCUS** on God. Jesus makes clear that we don't fast so that others will think we're spiritual. And Jesus doesn't tell us to fast for physical health benefits. Those benefits may exist, but Jesus tells us to fast because we want to know and enjoy God more than we want anything else in this world, even more than we want the basic daily necessity of food.

As we focus on God in fasting, we **ABSTAIN** from food. We set aside food for a meal or a day or multiple days as a discipline to say, "God, more than I want food, I want you. Your Word is my daily bread. I need your mercy more than I need a meal. I want your kingdom to come and your will to be done more than I want my stomach to be full."

Instead of eating, we then **SUBSTITUTE** the time we would be eating with prayer and God's Word. Fasting is not just skipping a meal. It's setting aside extra time to spend with God instead of eating. In this sense, fasting is feasting. Instead of having a normal meal, we pray and meditate on God's Word. Then all throughout the day whenever we're hungry, we say, "God, more than I want to enjoy food right now (which I really want!), I want to know and enjoy you."

As we fast, we will **TASTE** and see that God is good. This is a direct quote from Psalm 34:8–10:

Oh, taste and see that the Lord is good! Blessed is the man who takes refuge in him! Oh, fear the Lord, you his saints, for those who fear him have no lack! The young lions suffer want and hunger, but those who seek the Lord lack no good thing.

As good as food is—in addition to countless other good things in the world—God is better. He's the Giver of every good gift, and it is good to seek and be satisfied in him alone.

FOR CONTEMPLATION AND DISCUSSION

It is indescribably good to walk with God through prayer and fasting. Both of these disciplines open the door to deep enjoyment of God in all of his glory and exaltation of him among the nations. In light of Jesus' invitation to pray and fast, and in light of Jesus' expectation that we pray and fast, I encourage you to ask and discuss with others the following questions:

What are 1–3 specific ways God is calling you to enjoy and exalt him more through prayer?

What are 1–3 specific ways God is calling you to enjoy and exalt him more through fasting?

As you answer these questions, don't forget that Jesus has promised you divine reward. Put what God is saying into practice and be confident that you will not regret it.

08

WALKING WITH GOD THROUGH HIS WORD

08
WALKING WITH GOD THROUGH HIS WORD

In the last chapter, we explored how walking with God through prayer and fasting opens the door wide every day throughout the day for you and me to enjoy God in all of his glory and exalt God among all of the nations. In this chapter, I want to show you one more discipline that is foundational to walking with God each day: meditation on his Word.

It's interesting that the Bible doesn't talk about reading God's Word as much as it talks about meditating on it. David writes in Psalm 1:1–2,

> *Blessed is the man who walks not in the counsel of the wicked, nor stands in the way of sinners, nor sits in the seat of scoffers; but his delight is in the law of the Lord, and on his law he meditates day and night.*

What does it mean, then, to meditate on God's Word?

OBSESSED

I think about when Heather and I first started dating in high school and she used to write me letters. This was before texting, social media, or email, so I would receive this piece of paper on which she had written, and words cannot describe the elation I felt holding it in my hand. I devoured every word.

Dear David. . .

Dear. What did she mean by that? Was she just casually starting a letter that way, or was I really dear to her? She did seem to like me. I read on.

I hope you've had a good day. ☺

I would look at that smiley face and wonder, "Why did she put that at the end of that sentence at that point?" I'd picture her smile as I continued reading.

I've been praying for you.

I would pause and ponder, "In what way is she praying for me? Is she praying for me like she prays for a lot of people? Or is she praying for me like she prays for her future husband?"

Needless to say, it took me a long time to get through even the shortest of letters. I was soaking in every word and phrase, reflecting on exactly what she was saying, thinking, feeling, and meaning. You might say that sounds pretty obsessive, and I might agree with you because I was in love. But that's kind of the point.

As followers of Jesus, we are in a love relationship with God. We are made to enjoy God, which means we delight in hearing his voice and soaking in his words. We want to know what he's saying, thinking, feeling, and meaning. We're obsessed.

Does this sound like your approach to God's Word?

MAPS

God's Word is like a cave filled with treasure. Psalm 119:162 puts it this way:

I rejoice at your word like one who finds great spoil.

What a great verse. God's Word is filled with spoil just waiting to be discovered and enjoyed.

Let's make the connection with all we've been seeing. How do we enjoy God in all of his glory and exalt God among all nations? By meditating on his Word and mining it for treasure, then living according to the spoil we find and sharing that spoil with others right around us and far from us.

Similar to how I gave you an acrostic for prayer and fasting, here is an acrostic for what it means to enjoy God's Word each day: **MAPS**. Imagine a treasure map that helps you mine the wonders of God's

Word in relationship with him.

MEDITATE AND MEMORIZE

M stands for **MEDITATE AND MEMORIZE**. Read the Bible every day. I strongly encourage you to use a daily Bible reading plan. I use one developed a couple of centuries ago by Robert Murray M'Cheyne. I read two chapters a day (usually one chapter from the Old Testament and another chapter from the New Testament or Psalms), and over the course of two years, I read through the Old Testament once and the New Testament and Psalms twice. Years ago, Heather and I started using this plan in our time alone with God each day, and it revolutionized our marriage. Now our kids do it with us, and our church family has done it together. It is so helpful to be in relationship with others who are walking with God together in his Word this way.

Regardless of what plan you might use, set aside a regular time in your day, or multiple times in your day (morning and evening, like Psalm 1 talks about), to meditate on God's Word. Much like I approached Heather's letters to me, read God's Word slowly, humbly, prayerfully, and reflectively. The goal is not to check off a box but to know and enjoy God.

Ask questions like, "What is this passage saying? What is happening? Who wrote this? Who first read this? Who are the main characters? What is happening in the story? What's the flow of the passage? What is the author saying (both the human author and ultimately the divine author)? Why did the author say it this way? What words are repeated or seem most important?"

Along the way, ask big picture questions like, "What is this passage teaching about who God is and how God works? What is this passage teaching about who we are (or more personally, who I am)? What is this passage teaching about who Jesus is and what it means to follow him?"

Meditate in all of these ways and then memorize. Memorization is one of the most practical, helpful ways to meditate as we repeat something over and over again until it becomes second nature to us, hidden deep in our hearts and minds.

Some people say, "I just don't memorize well." I certainly realize that different people have different capacities to memorize, but let me ask you a question. What if I told you that I would give you $1,000 for every verse you could memorize between now and this time tomorrow?

I'm guessing you could learn to memorize a few verses. John 11:35 says, "Jesus wept." Just like that, you'd have $1,000. I'm pretty confident that you could memorize a good number of verses if money like that was on the line.

Now listen to Psalm 119:72. David writes,

The law of your mouth is better to me than thousands of gold and silver pieces.

Is that true? That seems to be the real question. Not whether you can memorize, but what is worth more to you: money or the Word of God?

As you meditate on a passage, pick a verse (or more) to memorize. I guarantee you that the more you meditate on and memorize God's Word, the more your life will count for what matters most. Isaiah 40:8 says,

The grass withers, the flower fades, but the word of our God will stand forever.

If you want to live for what's going to last forever, then meditate on and memorize the Word that lasts forever.

APPLY

After meditating on and memorizing God's Word, **APPLY** what you've heard from God. Think about the concentric circles we talked about earlier and ask how God's Word affects every facet of your life:

HEART: How does this passage change your heart?

MIND: How does this passage change what you think?

AFFECTIONS: How does this passage change what you desire?

WILL: How does this passage change what you do?

RELATIONSHIPS: How does this passage change the way you interact with others?

PURPOSE: How does this passage change your life to be more in line with God's purpose?

Take time to consider intentionally how God's Word transforms you from the inside out.

PRAY
Then **PRAY** God's Word. Remember the acrostic for praying and consider how God's Word leads you to pray:

How does this passage lead you to PRAISE God?

How does this passage lead you to REPENT of sin?

What does this passage lead you to ASK God for in your life and in others' lives?

How does this passage lead you to YIELD to God?

Jesus says in John 15:7,

If you abide in me, and my words abide in you, ask whatever you wish, and it will be done for you.

That's a promise from Jesus that when we pray according to his Word, he will answer us. With that kind of guarantee from God himself, let's pray his Word and watch how he responds in our lives and in the world.

SHARE

Finally, **SHARE** what you see and learn in God's Word. I strongly encourage you to write down your personal reflections on God's Word. I find it very helpful to write out what I'm seeing in God's Word, how it applies to my life, and the different ways it leads me to pray.

Then look for opportunities to encourage others with what you've read. Remember this is at the core of what it means to make disciples: sharing, showing, and teaching God's Word to others. Don't let God's Word stop with you; let God's Word spread through you.

I remember preaching a sermon once where I finished by asking that question: "Will God's Word stop with you or spread through you?" The next week, a young guy came up to me and said, "That question really hit home with me." Then he pulled up his sleeve to show me a tattoo he had gotten on his arm that week that said, "Will the Word stop with me or spread through me?"

I'm not advocating tattooing this on your skin, but I am encouraging you to imprint this on your heart. God's Word is too good to keep to yourself.

FOR CONTEMPLATION AND DISCUSSION

As someone made to enjoy God in all of his glory and exalt God in all of the world, I encourage you to meditate on and memorize his Word. Apply it. Pray it. Then share it with others.

Similar to the questions about prayer and fasting in your life, ask and discuss with others:

What are 1–3 specific ways God is calling you to enjoy and exalt him more through meditation on his Word?

As you put what God is saying to you into practice in your life, I pray that you will grow in your obsession with the Word of God because you are growing in your love and enjoyment of God himself.

09
GOSPEL THREADS

09
GOSPEL THREADS

A friend of mine who is now with the Lord was once living on the front lines of a red zone in the world. He and his family had moved to a dangerous place for any Christian to live, and particularly dangerous for anyone to become a Christian. But my friend and his family were faithfully sharing the gospel at the risk of their lives, and people were coming to faith in Jesus.

As soon as someone became a follower of Jesus, my friend would have an initial conversation with this new Christian about the cost not just of following Jesus, but of obeying Jesus' command to make disciples. My friend would ask him or her to make a list of all the people they know—to write down the names of family members, friends, neighbors, co-workers, etc. Then my friend would ask this new Christian to circle the names of the five people who were least likely to kill them if they shared the gospel with them. After circling those names, my friend would help this new Christian start to share the gospel with those five people.

Sharing the gospel with others, no matter what it costs, was one of the first things my friend taught new Christians. Why? Because this is foundational to what it means to follow Jesus. Sharing the gospel is so foundational to faith that it's worth risking our lives to do from the very beginning of the Christian life.

But here's the problem. Most Christians don't actively share the gospel with other people, even years after becoming a follower of Jesus. We are missing out on one of the foundational parts of the Christian life, and it's clear evidence that we're not enjoying God in all of his glory and exalting God among all of the nations. We share what we most enjoy, and we can't exalt God if we don't tell others about him.

Satan likes it this way. He is our adversary, and he is doing everything he can to keep us from experiencing God's purpose for our lives while also keeping others from hearing about God's love in their lives. This is why Paul, when he talks about spiritual warfare in Ephesians 6:18–20, says,

> To that end, keep alert with all perseverance, making supplication for all the saints, and also for me, that words may be given to me in opening my mouth boldly to proclaim the mystery of the gospel, for which I am an ambassador in chains, that I may declare it boldly, as I ought to speak.

In this chapter, I want to encourage and pray for your boldness in sharing the gospel with people around you. In addition, I want to help you with a simple way to share the gospel in your ordinary, everyday life.

WEAVING THE GOSPEL

Journey with me to another country in a red zone of the world, specifically in the Middle East. It's illegal in this country to share the gospel with Muslims, and conversion to Christianity is outlawed. Yet I know a small group of Christians there who are making disciples every single day in a very simple way.

These believers run a business that employs Muslim men and women, and in the course of working and living alongside Muslims all day long, they work intentionally to, in their words, "weave gospel threads" into the fabric of their interactions with their co-workers. In every conversation, business interaction, meeting, and meal, they look for opportunities to speak about who God is, how God loves us, what God is doing in the world, and ultimately what God has done for us in Jesus.

This doesn't mean that every conversation they have is a full-on, hour-long gospel explanation. Instead, they try to saturate all of their normal conversations with various strands of the gospel, like weaving colored threads into a quilt. Their prayer is that over time, God will open the eyes of the Muslims around them to behold the tapestry of the gospel that has been woven in front of them, and they will come to Jesus.

I remember first watching this gospel-weaving in action, and I was amazed at how natural (or better put, supernatural) gospel sharing can be in casual interactions, whether in workplaces or in homes. I listened to brothers and sisters in Christ share stories about Jesus and truth from God's Word. I sat in a shop where my friend Mark was talking with a Muslim shop owner and sharing about how Jesus was working in his life and family that week. Another time, while we were waiting to eat dinner with a Muslim family in their home, I listened to my friend Kim share about the selfless love God has for us.

Late one night, I found myself with Robert talking with a group of men about the divinity of Jesus. That's a major obstacle to coming to Christ for many Muslims. I must admit that I was a bit nervous as we sat in an upstairs room late at night surrounded by Muslims I'd just met in a country where it's illegal to share the gospel, and we were discussing what could be the most contentious, provocative, even insulting truth in the gospel for Muslims. But these men were open to listening because of the way that people like Mark, Kim, and Robert loved them and lived among them.

These believers who worked together in this business had earned the right to be heard. They were honest in their work. They honored the people with whom they worked. They cared for each other and for the people around them. When other employees went through hard times, these brothers and sisters showed God's love to them. When co-workers were sick or in need, these brothers and sisters asked if they could pray for them. Most of the time, their co-workers were glad to have others pray for them. As these Christians prayed in Jesus' name, Muslim men and women saw a visual picture of God's goodness that matched all the times they had heard different things about Jesus.

As a result of all this, people were coming to faith in Jesus. Muslims would secretly pull believers aside to ask more questions about who Jesus is and how Jesus saves. One by one, God was drawing co-workers, their families, and their neighbors to himself. They were being baptized and becoming a church.

In other words, disciples were being made among the nations through followers of Jesus weaving gospel threads in everyday conversations. As I think about Mark, Kim, and Robert, just ordinary followers of Jesus working alongside one another and living to make disciples, I can't help but wonder, "Why don't we all do this in our everyday lives wherever we live, go to school, work, and play?"

GOSPEL

In this chapter, I want to encourage you to think about six threads of the gospel and how you can weave them into your everyday interactions and conversations. At the risk of overwhelming you with acrostics, I'm going to give you one more to help you remember the **GOSPEL** as you think about how to share it every day.

Start with **GOD'S CHARACTER**. In your conversations with people around you every day at school, work, the gym, or anywhere else, talk about God as someone you know, worship, and love. Don't talk like an atheist, attributing circumstances to chance or coincidence. Talk about who God is, how God is working, and how thankful you are for his goodness in the world, his provision in your life, and so on.

Then talk about the **OFFENSE OF SIN**. You're probably not going to walk up to a classmate, co-worker, or neighbor today and tell them they're a dreadful sinner in need of salvation. But you can speak humbly and seriously about sin in your life or evil in the world. You can talk about the effects of sin, suffering, pain, evil, and death around us. You can point people to the reality that things are not as they should be in the world, and you can share how this is a result of our separation from God.

Then look for opportunities to talk about the **SUFFICIENCY OF JESUS**. Talk about Jesus like you know him (because you do!). Talk about how he is your peace and joy in a world of sin, suffering, pain, evil, and death. When an opportunity presents itself, tell some of your favorite stories about Jesus' life, including truths he taught, people he healed, miracles he performed, and ways he served. Then talk about his death. Do the people around you know how grateful you are that Jesus gave his life for you? Finally, talk about the hope you have because of Jesus' resurrection from the grave. Every difficulty, challenge, or trial you and I face in this world is an opportunity to point others around us to the one who has overcome this world.

Look for opportunities to talk about a **PERSONAL RESPONSE** to Jesus. Share with as many people as you can about how your life changed the moment you put your faith in Jesus. Tell people that God wants them to experience a personal relationship with him, and that they can begin a relationship with him at any point in their lives. Talk with people about what it means to have faith that leads to forgiveness of sin and freedom from futile, endless efforts to find satisfaction apart from relationship with God.

At some point in your conversations with others around you, talk about the **ETERNAL URGENCY** of faith in Jesus. Do we realize that every day we are talking, texting, chatting, posting, and interacting with people who are all going to spend eternity either in heaven or hell? Surely at some point we need to go deeper in our conversations than weather, food, sports, and the like. Talk with people about the reality that this world and all that is in it will not last. Ask people if they know what will happen to them when they die, knowing that could be any day for any one of us. None of us is guaranteed tomorrow. How does that change the way we talk today?

Finally, talk about the **LIFE TRANSFORMATION** that Jesus brings. Remember Mark, Kim, and Robert in that Muslim country. People listened to them share the gospel because their lives reflected the transformation the gospel brings. Share and show how your life is better as a result of faith in Jesus. Obviously "better" doesn't mean "easier." That certainly isn't the case for followers of Jesus in red zones, and it's not guaranteed to be the case for anyone in green zones, either. But share and show the supernatural difference Jesus has made in your life and encourage others with all the ways Jesus desires to change their lives for good.

FOR CONTEMPLATION AND DISCUSSION

As we close this chapter, I want to encourage you to make a list of people in your life who, as best as you can tell, don't know Jesus. Then consider and discuss with others how you can begin to intentionally weave gospel threads into the fabric of your everyday conversations and interactions with those specific people:

How can you weave GOD'S CHARACTER into the fabric of your everyday conversations?

How can you weave the OFFENSE OF SIN into the fabric of your everyday conversations?

How can you weave the SUFFICIENCY OF JESUS into
the fabric of your everyday conversations?

How can you weave PERSONAL RESPONSE to Jesus into
the fabric of your everyday conversations?

How can you weave ETERNAL URGENCY into the fabric
of your everyday conversations?

How can you weave the LIFE TRANSFORMATION
that Jesus brings into the fabric of your everyday
conversations?

Pray intentionally for boldness to weave the gospel into
your everyday interactions. Then pray that God will open
the eyes of the people on your list (as well as others around
you) to see the tapestry of the gospel woven through your
life and words, and pray that they might receive his love in
their lives.

10

THE LIFE THAT THAT COUNTS

10
THE LIFE THAT COUNTS

What is God's will for my life?

This is one of the most common questions I hear from Christians. We make so many decisions over the course of our lives, and many (if not most) of them are not specifically addressed in the Bible. Some of these decisions are small and seemingly insignificant. Others are large and life-altering.

Should I get married? If so, who should I marry? Should we have children? If so, how many children? What career path should I pursue? Where should I live? How should I live? We make so many decisions that we can find ourselves constantly wondering, "How do I find God's will?"

I hope that by now you realize there's no need to "find" God's will—because he's not hiding it from you. God has made his will for our lives crystal clear in his Word. Just put together everything we have seen so far.

God's will for your life, revealed from cover to cover in his Word, is for you to enjoy God in all of his glory and exalt God among all of the nations. God wants you to experience his will so much that he has put his Holy Spirit inside of you to make you more and more like Jesus every day. As you follow Jesus, God's will is for you to make disciples of the nations in a world where over 3 billion people still haven't been reached with the gospel. God's will is for you to walk with him in this world through prayer, fasting, meditation on his Word, and sharing his Word with others, weaving the gospel into the fabric of your everyday conversations. As you live this way, you won't find God's will for your life; you'll experience it.

In this final chapter, I want to show you how God will call you to experience his will for your life in unique, creative, beautiful, and un-imaginable ways.

CALLING

Let's look back at a passage we read previously, Acts 13:1–3:

Now there were in the church at Antioch prophets and teachers, Barnabas, Simeon who was called Niger, Lucius of Cyrene, Manaen a lifelong friend of Herod the tetrarch, and Saul. While they were worshiping the Lord and fasting, the Holy Spirit said, "Set apart for me Barnabas and Saul for the work to which I have called them." Then after fasting and praying they laid their hands on them and sent them off.

Pay close attention to these words from the Holy Spirit, for they show us a picture of God's specific calling in two people's lives. This call from the Holy Spirit was unique, setting apart Barnabas and Saul

THE LIFE THAT COUNTS

in a way that was different from all the other Christians at Antioch. Based on this passage and other places in Scripture, let's think about God's call in our lives in four ways.

First, think about God's **call to salvation**. This is actually the primary way that God's Word talks about *calling*. God graciously calls us into relationship with him through faith in Jesus. If you are a Christian, think about the time when God specifically called you to faith in Jesus. Someone somehow shared the gospel with you, and by the power of God's Spirit at work in your heart, he called you to himself. When you think about Acts 13, God had done that for all the Christians at Antioch.

Related to God's call to salvation is God's **call to mission** in our lives. Everyone God calls to salvation God also calls to mission. We saw this in Jesus' words in Matthew 4:19:

Follow me, and I will make you fishers of men.

The call to follow Jesus was at the same time a call to fish for men. As we've seen, the call to be a disciple of Jesus is a call to make disciples of all nations. This was God's call for every Christian at Antioch.

The same is true for each of us. Regardless of where we live, how we're gifted, or what we do, we are all disciple-makers of the nations. Each of us is personally called by God to love others as ourselves by laying down our lives to lead our neighbors in all nations to Jesus.

This leads to a third picture of *calling* that we see in God's Word: his **call to station** in our lives. By *station*, I'm referring to the different roles and positions to which God may call us. One example of a station in your life might be your role in a family. God may call you to be a son or daughter, brother or sister, husband or wife, mom or dad, or grandparent. If God has called you to one of those positions in a family, then God has called you to enjoy him and exalt him through your role as a faithful family member according to his Word. God calls some Christians to enjoy and exalt him among the nations through marriage and others through singleness, either for a period of time or the entirety of one's life. God specifically called Saul (or Paul) to singleness, a calling he describes more in depth in 1 Corinthians 7.

As another example of God's call to station in our lives, God calls you and me to be a part, or member, of a particular local church. Or God may call you or me to be a citizen of a particular country. Now we're starting to see that while God calls all Christians alike to salvation and mission, his call to different stations varies between our lives. Different Christians have different roles in a family, and not all Christians are members of the same local church or citizens of the same country.

All of this leads to the fourth way we see God's call in our lives: a **call to service**. This is specifically what we see happening in the beginning of Acts 13. Notice that God didn't call everybody in the church at Antioch to pack their bags and travel to another place for the spread of the gospel. Instead, God left most of them in Antioch as he called Saul and Barnabas to leave Antioch. That didn't mean that Paul and Barnabas were super-Christians who really cared about the nations while everyone else who stayed at Antioch was just an average

THE LIFE THAT COUNTS   109

Christian who didn't care about the nations. It simply meant that God called different people to make disciples of the nations in different ways.

The same will be true for us. God calls you and me to carry out his mission to make disciples of all nations in different ways at different times among different people in different locations through different vocations. What's important to remember is that all of us, not just certain people, are called to be disciple-makers of the nations. What differentiates us is where and in what ways God *calls* us to do this.

THE CREATIVITY OF GOD

The creativity of God's calling in each of our lives is exhilarating to contemplate. I think about different people of different ages with different gifts and skills in different parts of the world, and I wonder about all the unique ways God will lead each of us to exalt him among all the nations. God will call some of you to be single and others of you to be married, and your singleness or marriage will be a unique part of how you fulfill God's purpose in your life.

Similarly, God will call most of us who are reading this book to work in different vocations with different gifts and opportunities that he provides. But we'll all have the same purpose: to enjoy God *as* we work and to exalt God *through* our work. Just imagine it. Teachers and medical professionals, investors and entrepreneurs, business leaders and day laborers, students and retirees all making disciples of Jesus wherever they live, work, and play. Then imagine them all looking for opportunities to do the same thing not just in green zones, but in red zones all over the world.

Much like God was doing at Antioch, he will call some of us to go to red zones in the world to reach people with the gospel. He'll lead us there for different amounts of time through different avenues of school, work, or otherwise. At the same time, God will call some of us to live in green zones and work from there for the spread of the gospel not only in the green zones, but also in the red zones. While the Holy Spirit will call us to serve in different ways, he will empower us all to make disciples of the nations.

FOR CONTEMPLATION AND DISCUSSION

As we come to a close, I want to summarize the foundational purpose of your life in one sentence:

You are made to enjoy God in all of his glory and exalt God among all of the nations by walking with God and becoming more like Jesus every day through prayer, fasting, meditating on his Word, and making disciples in the power of the Holy Spirit.

When you live for this purpose however, wherever, whenever, and in whatever unique ways God calls you, your life will count for what matters most.

Think about or look back to all the questions you answered at the end of previous chapters. Then consider your life today, and answer the question,

How am I going to live each day for what matters most?

Specifically consider and discuss with others:

How am I going to live to enjoy God in all of his glory?

How am I going to live to exalt God among all the nations?

Knowing there is an adversary in this world who wants you to waste your life and who wants to keep God's glory from spreading in the world, I want to exhort you in the name of Jesus: live for this purpose. Die for this purpose. Realize this is the foundation of full, eternal life, and don't settle for anything less. And one day, you and I will find ourselves by God's grace before God's throne, surrounded by people from every nation, tribe, and language, and together with them we will enjoy and exalt God for all of eternity.

[1] See *Don't Hold Back: Leaving Behind the American Gospel to Follow Jesus Fully* and *Radical: Taking Back Your Faith from the American Dream.*

[2] You should be able to find this Bible reading plan by searching for "Robert Murray M'Cheyne Bible Reading Plan" through any web browser. D.A. Carson has also written an excellent two-volume companion devotional to this Bible reading plan called *For the Love of God.* I use it most every day (and have for years) and would highly recommend it to you.

ABOUT DAVID PLATT

David Platt serves as a pastor in metro Washington, D.C. He is the founder of Radical.

David received his Ph.D. from New Orleans Baptist Theological Seminary and is the author of *Don't Hold Back, Radical, Follow Me, Counter Culture, Something Needs to Change, Before You Vote,* as well as multiple volumes of the *Christ-Centered Exposition Commentary* series.

Along with his wife and children, David lives in the Washington, D.C., metro area.

ABOUT RADICAL

Jesus calls us to make his glory known among all the nations by making disciples and multiplying churches. Being on mission is not a program, but the calling of our lives as Christians.

However 3.2 billion people are currently unreached with the gospel, and many of them endure unimaginable suffering. And, only 1% of missions dollars and 3% of missionaries go to the unreached. Something has to change.

Radical exists to equip Christians to be on mission. We serve the church by equipping Christians to **follow Jesus** and to **make him known** in their neighborhoods and among all nations. In places where the gospel is already accessible, we work to **awaken** and **mobilize** the church. In areas where access is limited, we work to **advance the gospel** and **see churches planted.**

ARTICLES, MESSAGES, SECRET CHURCH ARCHIVES, VIDEOS & MORE

RADICAL.NET

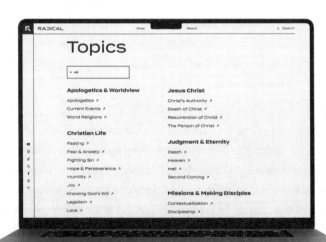

APPAREL WITH PURPOSE

100% of the proceeds of every item sold go to support church planting, humanitarian relief, leadership training, and resource development for the spread of the gospel to those who have never heard it.

SHOP.RADICAL.NET

NEIGHBORHOODS
& NATIONS

A DOCUMENTARY SERIES EXAMINING GOD'S WORK
IN DIFFICULT PLACES AROUND THE WORLD

YOUTUBE.COM/@FOLLOWRADICAL

RADICAL BOOKSTORE

Find best-sellers at discount prices like David Platt's books *Radical* and *Something Needs to Change* as well as other faith-based resources to help deepen your spiritual journey.

MAKE CHRIST KNOWN AMONG THE UNREACHED

Through Urgent, Radical supports the faithful and effective work of national believers through and for the local church among the unreached in places with the most urgent spiritual and physical needs.

RADICAL.NET/URGENT   GIVE TODAY!

NOTES

NOTES

NOTES